Horses
Sally Gordon

CHARTWELL BOOKS INC.

Designed and produced by
Albany Books
36 Park Street London W1Y 4DE

First published 1979

Published by Chartwell Books Inc.
A Division of Book Sales Inc.
110 Enterprise Avenue
Secaucus, New Jersey 07094

Copyright © Albany Books 1979

Printed in Hong Kong

Picture research: Mary Corcoran

Contents

Pages 4 & 5: *Horses are gregarious animals. When turned out in a field they appreciate some company, even if it is only to help satisfy an annoying itch!* (Peter Roberts)

Pages 6 & 7: *The work of a police horse is not always unpleasant. Here one stops for a moment to make friends with a young member of the public.* (Police Federation)

Endpapers: *Trotters race towards the camera on a snow-covered track in St Moritz.* (ZEFA)

The Wild Horse

Like all living animals, the horse has evolved into the noble beast we know today through centuries of gradual change and variation. It began its life some 60 million years ago as a small creature only about 30 cm (12 ins) tall; and it was not just in its diminutive size that it bore little resemblance to today's horse. Its back was convex rather than concave, it had a tiny head, a long bony tail, and perhaps most significantly of all, four toes on its forefeet and three on its hind. The fossilized remains of this creature, known as *Eohippus,* have been found in northern Europe and in the vicinity of the Mississippi River, indicating that it was indigenous to Eurasia and North America. It is generally accepted however, that it originated in the southern part of what is now the United States of America and from there migrated across the land bridges that at that time united this part of the world with northern Europe.

During the geological epochs that pre-dated the appearance of man on earth, the horse passed through a number of evolutionary changes. Successive types showed subtle variations in conformation in order to adapt to the ever-changing nature of the surrounding environment. As each new adaptation became no longer suited to the terrain, vegetation or climatic conditions, that particular animal would die out, to be replaced by another that showed more advanced characteristics. Gradually an animal evolved in which the spinal column had become almost horizontal, and the legs had become longer and stronger so that as a non-aggressive creature it was able to escape its predators by speed. As grass took the place of leaves in the diet, the animal's teeth became flatter and those of a grazing, as opposed to a browsing, herbivore. And as the ground became firmer, the fourth toe on the forefeet

Below: *Primitive wild horses known as* Equus caballus. *Some still live wild, but more will be found in the major zoos of the world.* (ZEFA)

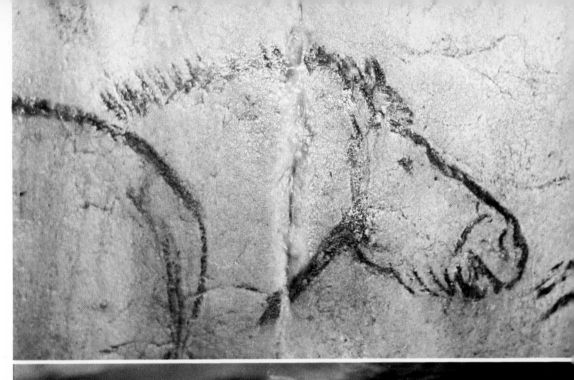

Pages 8 & 9: *Equally at home knee-deep in water or on drier land, these Camargue ponies find grazing and nourishment where they can.* (ZEFA)

Right: *Compare the prehistoric cave painting of a pony's head found at the Grotte de Nieux in the Hautes Pyrénnés, France, with the photograph taken recently of the head of a Przewalski's Horse yearling. The similarity is startling.* (Joyce Pope)

Left: *A Przewalski mare and foal grazing. The dun coat colour and the striped 'bar' or zebra markings seen behind the knees on the mare's legs are signs of primitive ancestry.* (Peter Roberts)

Right: *Today, Mustangs are most frequently seen in rodeo rings as the 'stars' of the bucking bronco events.* (US Travel Service)

Below: *The wild Mustangs, once a common feature of the American plains, were always the mounts of the Indians. Here they are depicted in a painting by George Catlin.* (Mansell Collection)

Above: *The Exmoor pony is the oldest of all the native breeds of the British Isles. It is said to be the pony the ancient Celts used to pull their war chariots.* (Peter Roberts)

Left: *The Shetland pony is considered the strongest of all breeds for its size. It is capable of pulling twice its own weight.* (Peter Roberts)

disappeared, the centre toe on both hind and forefeet developed into a hoof, and the other two toes shrank so that they no longer touched the ground. The first truly monodactyl or fully-hoofed animal, known as *Pliohippus,* appeared during the Pliocene period that extended from ten to one million BC.

By the time man had emerged, *Pliohippus* had evolved into *Equus Caballus,* an animal which is completely recognizable as the horse we know today. Like its earliest ancestors, it appears to have originated in North America and subsequently migrated across to Europe and Asia.

Nowadays, there are something in excess of two hundred breeds of horses and ponies in existence throughout the world. Many of these have been created by man, who as he learned about animal husbandry and the art of selective breeding, was able to cross breeds with one another to produce animals best suited to his many and various needs. Many other breeds, however, are native or indigenous to a particular area or country and have existed there for centuries, breeding and surviving naturally, virtually unbothered or unaided by man. There is disagreement among prehistorians as to whether all these native breeds evolved from *Equus Caballus* alone or from a number of wild species of horse that existed after the Ice Age.

Those who claim that there has been only one primordial ancestor liken it to a breed of horse, or more particularly, pony (the distinction really being only one of size), that still exists today. This is *Equus Przewalskii,* a creature which certainly bears a very strong resemblance to primitive cave drawings that have been found in a number of places around the world. It is a thick-set, somewhat coarse-looking animal, with a rough, woolly coat and a scrubby mane and tail. Existing in the wild only in the western area of the Gobi Desert, it was generally thought to be extinct, until a herd was discovered by a Russian explorer, Colonel Przewalski, in the latter part of the nineteenth century.

To describe *Equus Przewalskii* (more commonly known as Przewalski's Horse), or indeed almost any horse or pony today as 'wild' is not strictly accurate, for certainly all types and breeds have at some stage been domesticated to varying degrees by man. Most of those that do still live 'wild', that is roaming free and fending for themselves through summer and winter, come under man's auspices in some way, and most 'wild' horses and ponies do in fact belong to somebody.

Some wild or feral horses have descended from entirely domesticated stock and are not, therefore, true native breeds. A good example of this is the Mustang of America which is still found roaming wild in such places as the Pryor Mountains on the borders of Montana and Wyoming. Although the horse as a species originated in America, for reasons that have never been indisputably established it became extinct there some time after the coming of *Equus Caballus*. Horses were not known again in America until the early sixteenth century when Cortez and his Spanish conquistadors brought them across on their conquering quest.

The horses brought by Cortez were, not surprisingly, of Spanish origin and were probably related to the stately Andalusians of which Spain is justly proud. The horses proved so useful in day-to-day living that they were encouraged to breed prolifically. Before long, the American Indians of the plains began to steal the horses, a 'profession' in which they became so proficient that the numbers they stole soon far exceeded the numbers they could use. The horses were then turned out to graze on the wild pampas land and rounded up by the Indians as they were wanted. Many roamed far afield and escaped re-capture and it was from these 'plains drifters' that the wild Mustang emerged.

Faced with hostile conditions of environment — poor vegetation and intemperate climate — only the fittest,

The Dartmoor pony is a near neighbour of the Exmoor and shares a similar, bleak moorland home. (ZEFA)

toughest, and most cunning survived to perpetuate the race. Consequently, in a very short time, the Mustang showed little of the tall, proud stature of its ancestors. Instead, it became rather undistinguished to look at — lightweight in build and bone structure, and somewhat plain. However, it adapted superbly to the rigours of its habitat, and its hardiness, combined with its versatility and agility, made it a favourite mount of the western cowboys, just as it had been of the Indians. Those horses whose nature proves really intractable, usually as a result of bad treatment at the hands of a particularly rough rider, are often relegated to the role of the 'bucking bronc' of the rodeo circuit. Whether this is in fact a retrogression is debatable, for some people say that such rodeo mounts are the most spoilt and pampered horses of all. It is certainly true that their period of 'working' time each year often amounts to little more than five minutes!

Mustangs used to roam the huge expanses of pampas, prairie and mountain foothills in their thousands. In fact at the beginning of the nineteenth

Constant grazing by the side of the road makes New Forest ponies immune to the roar of traffic. (Peter Roberts)

century there were estimated to be about two million wild Mustangs. Now there are thought to be less than ten thousand — a decline owed entirely to man's exploitation of them. Over the decades we have hunted and killed the Mustang for all manner of reasons — to make into chicken feed or fertilizer or to remove it from valuable land. Fortunately laws have now been passed to protect the remaining Mustangs.

On the other side of the world, in the outback areas of Australia, the wild Brumbies roam. Like the Mustangs, they are the feral descendants of domesticated stock. They were turned loose on the ranges while their owners went in search of gold during the mid-nineteenth century gold rush. So successfully did the wily Brumby breed that it became a pest to farmers and homesteaders. People find their fences torn down, their pastures trampled, their precious water reserves depleted

Left: *Highland ponies photographed on the Island of Rhum, Scotland. The thick, plentiful mane and long, full tail that are characteristics of the breed are well illustrated here.* (ARDEA)

Below: *Fell ponies are said to be descended from horses brought to Britain by the Romans.* (C. A. Visual)

and even their domestic horses enticed away to a life of freedom. As a result, a systematic programme of rounding-up the Brumbies and destroying them was put into operation in the 1960s, so that now their numbers are very much diminished. 'Brumby' is an Australian word for 'wild horse' and Brumbies do have a reputation for being genuinely 'wild' in temperament. Attempts to tame or train those that have been brought into captivity have rarely been successful.

The British Isles have nine indigenous pony breeds. All may still be seen roaming free in their particular areas, although all will also be found in domestic circumstances as they make excellent riding ponies. They have in common an inherent hardiness, an amazing sure-footedness that comes from generations of contending with rough or rocky terrain, and an ability to withstand the hardships of their environment. The tough, diminutive Shetlands,

for example, which inhabit the islands of the same name to the north of Scotland, have learnt such tricks as scrounging fish heads from the fishermen. These sustain them through the winter when there is little else to eat. Similarly, the Exmoor ponies that roam the bleak moors in south-west England supplement their meagre diet by digging up bracken tubers with their hooves, often pawing their way through a thick crust of snow to get to them. Exmoor ponies are said to be endowed with great intelligence and the shepherds of the moors claim they are much better able to survive the rigours of a hard winter than the sheep and deer with which they share their habitat. They appear to know instinctively that they must avoid the treacherous bogs that are a feature of the moors. After a wet spell, tempting though the emerald green grass looks, it is not to be crossed. Yet what is still more amazing is the way the ponies appear to know when the ground has dried out

Above: *Seen more frequently in its home in the English North Country than in the show ring as here, the Dales pony is often jet black in colour.* (Peter Roberts)

Right: *A Welsh Mountain pony mare and her foal. Grey is one of the commonest coat colours among this breed.* (Peter Roberts)

sufficiently to withstand their weight, and venture onto it to crop the lush grass.

Dartmoor and New Forest ponies, both found in the areas from which they take their names, have existed wild in these places for centuries. Both, however, have been subjected to doses of 'alien' blood over the generations, making them rather less pure as breeds and recognizable as types than some of the other native breeds. The Dartmoor got much of its admixture of blood from Shetland ponies. These were turned out on the moor with the aim of producing a small, hardy pony that would be ideal for working in coal mines. Similarly, towards the end of the nineteenth century, the New Forest pony interbred with various other native breeds that were let loose in the forest. The aim was to improve the breed. In fact, the introduction of blood caused a degeneration in the breeds and now

attempts are being made to establish a definite type in both cases.

The other native British pony breeds are the Highland ponies, of which there are various types living in the Highlands of Scotland and the outlying coastal Isles, the Fell and the Dales found respectively on the west and east of the Pennine range of hills in northern England, the pretty Welsh Mountain ponies from Wales and the Connemaras from Ireland. All roam their native areas in groups of two or three, but all are put into domestic use too; the Highland ponies are traditionally the ponies of the crofters, helping them in their day to day farming lives as well as being used to carry the deer carcases down from the mountains after a day's stalking; the Fell ponies were once much used as pack animals to carry lead from the mines to the coastal ports as well as making excellent harness ponies and farm workers, while the thick-set Dales,

Right: *A beautiful Connemara pony grazes among the rocky outcrops of its home in the Connaught Province of Ireland.* (Peter Roberts)

Below: *'Wild' Welsh Mountain ponies herded together in a small pen await their fate at a pony sale.* (Peter Roberts)

at one time slaughtered in their hundreds for meat, are now widely sought as trekking mounts. Welsh mountain ponies and Connemaras, being among the prettiest of the native breeds, are in demand world-wide as children's riding and show ponies. The Spanish blood that runs in the Connemara's veins and may in part account for its attractive appearance is said to owe its origins to the Spanish horses that escaped from the shipwrecked Armada in the late sixteenth century. It is claimed that the horses swam ashore and thereafter mated with the little local ponies that had roamed the area centuries before man set foot there.

The Shetland pony, incidentally, is not the smallest breed of pony in the world. That title must go to the Argentinian breed known as the Falabella, representatives of which stand under 7 hands high (70 cm/28 ins — a hand being equal to 10 cm/4 ins). Falabellas were developed as a breed by

an Argentinian family of that name in Buenos Aires within the last century.

The beautiful 'wild' Camargue ponies that live among the swamplands of the Rhône delta in south-eastern France, have to contend with vastly different conditions from those of the horses and ponies so far described. Their natural habitat is extremely marshy, cut across at frequent intervals by large expanses of water. Many ponies still live a life of freedom in this area and appear to be quite at ease splashing their way through the small rivers and lakes that crop up all around them. In the springtime, there is lush grazing for the ponies, but they have to stock up at this time of year, for during the autumn and winter the vegetation is extremely poor and sparse, with little nutritional value.

Camargue ponies are almost always grey in colour, although the foals are born black. As they mature, their soft baby coat gradually turns to grey and from then on with each successive annual moult, it gets lighter still. Old

Above: *The smallest pony in the world — the Falabella. An estimation of its height can be gauged by comparing it to the height of the fence and the gatepost in the picture.* (Peter Roberts)

Right: *Camargue ponies are branded with the initials or the heraldic family crest of their owner. The brand on the right flank of the pony shows clearly here.* (ZEFA)

Left: *The gardiens of the Camargue use the native ponies as their mounts in the annual round-up of the famous black bulls of the region.* (French Government Tourist Office)

Below left: *Thick, fluffy coats help these Dülmen ponies to face the bleak winter in their wooded home in Germany.* (ZEFA)

Below: *Known for its inherent docility and friendliness, the Icelandic pony is nevertheless also renowned for its independence. It is among the hardiest of all breeds.* (Solarfilma)

horses have almost pure white coats. The breed is a very ancient one, thought to have inhabited the area for many centuries. Cave drawings of primitive horses at Solutre and Lascaux bear a strong resemblance to today's Camargue ponies, and their similarity has given rise to the theory that today's ponies are descended from the prehistoric ones that clearly lived in these areas.

Besides those that run wild on the watery plains, many Camargue ponies are caught and trained to be mounts of the Camargue cowboys or *gardiens*. The horses are used in daily work as well as playing an important role in the local fêtes and carnivals. They help in the ceremonious annual round-up of the wild horses (for checking, culling and branding) as well as in the traditional round-up and stampede through the streets of the famous black bulls with which they share the area.

Germany still has one native pony, the

Dülmen, that is allowed to roam at least semi-wild. The Senner, which at one time also ran free in Germany, is now thought to be extinct; indeed, the 600-year old breed of Dülmen ponies is also considerably diminished in numbers. Just one herd is still in existence; it belongs to the Duke of Cröy and lives in a forested reserve in Westphalia.

Iceland, too, has a well-known native pony, representatives of which may still be seen roaming in semi-wild herds. For generations, however, the tough little ponies that were taken to the country by the first Norse settlers a thousand years ago have played a vital role in the lives of the Icelandic people. Many are still used to work on remote farms where the rugged terrain or inaccessibility makes it unsuitable or impossible for motor vehicles to venture. Icelandic ponies possess a rare homing instinct and will find their way back to their home pastures, unaided, over considerable distances. Exceptionally hardy, their winter diet includes lichen that they pick off the trees. Fishermen have to keep a wary eye on their catch if ponies are

about, for the animals are particularly partial to a breakfast of freshly-caught fish!

Doubtless there are various small herds of wild horses and ponies in existence in remote, little-known areas of the world. Mongolian ponies (similar in appearance to Przewalski's Horse) almost certainly still roam parts of Mongolia and China; there are wild horses about which very little is known, living on the inhospitable interior plateau of Sardinia; the island of Assateague that lies in the Atlantic Ocean off the coast of Virginia has a race of wild ponies said to have descended from others that were ship-wrecked on their way from North Africa to Peru some centuries ago, and there is a race of smokey-grey coloured, small horses or ponies which live along the banks of the River Niger in Africa. Many more will have disappeared, either brought in to domestic use or perished at the hands of man. It seems, therefore, that by and large we have to turn to the domestic horse for the future of the species as a whole.

The wild ponies that live generally unmolested on Assateague Island are rounded-up and swum across the narrow channel for the annual sales on the Island of Chincoteague. (US Travel Service)

The Riding Horse

It is not known for certain just when or by whom the horse was first domesticated, although mention of horses has been discovered on clay tablets known to date back as far as 3000-2000 BC. Man's first conception of the horse would, in any event, have been as a source of food. Not until he became aware of his own superior intelligence, which would allow him mastery over the animal, would he have used the horse to carry him or his belongings or draw his primitive sleds.

Although men undoubtedly did ride the small wild horses that roamed Eurasia in the second millenium BC, it would seem that the first definite records — in the form of pictures — to show men riding more impressive-looking horses are those found in an Egyptian tomb dating from the fourteenth century BC. A form of bridle with a bit had been devised by then to give greater control over the animal, but the saddle had not yet been invented.

The history of riding, through the centuries and throughout the world, has been studded with riding masters who have influenced style or in some way left

their mark. The first and probably still the most famous was the Greek cavalry officer, Xenophon, who lived in the fourth century BC. Although he and his officers rode without saddles, the position of the rider on the horse and the riding seat he recommended remained almost unchanged until the twentieth century.

In the centuries that followed Xenophon, the two factors that probably most affected and influenced riding were the invention of the horse-shoe and the firm saddle equipped with stirrups. The metal horseshoe was introduced during the first century AD and it meant horses could be ridden for longer periods, over all types of terrain, and at virtually any time of year with less danger of incurring injury to their feet. Riders had used a variety of saddle cloths almost since riding had begun, but most were little more than a thin pad, maybe held in place by a girth strapped round the horse's middle. The Scythians improved on this by adding two well-stuffed cushions which were joined by cross-straps and rested on either side of the horse's spine, while

Above: *Greek riders of about 450 BC depicted on the frieze of the Parthenon. These riders had no saddles or bridles to aid them and yet their riding position is similar to that practised today.* (Mansell Collection)

Above right: *The knights of the Norman Conquest, shown here on the famous Bayeux tapestry, rode with almost straight legs.* (Mansell Collection)

Right: *Classical equitation reached its zenith during the sixteenth and seventeenth centuries. In this painting by Baron Reis d'Eisenburg, a rider demonstrates the capriole.* (Peter Roberts)

Pages 30 & 31: *Even on a frosty morning, riders can still enjoy the beauty of the countryside from horseback.* (C. A. Visual)

Left: *The magnificent hall of the Spanish Riding School in Vienna where displays of classical equitation are regularly given using the famous white Lipizzaner stallions.* (Peter Roberts)

Below left: *That the movements of* haute école *were taught as tactics for war is well illustrated here. The black horse, centre, is performing a virtual levade.* (Mansell Collection)

Below right: *Until very recently, women always rode side-saddle. Their horses were generally lighter and more refined than those ridden by their male contemporaries.* (Mary Evans Picture Library)

their Eastern neighbours, the Sarmatians, appear to have used saddles which incorporated a proper 'tree' (the firm foundation of all modern saddles, whatever their exterior design). The invention of the stirrup, which may have existed in some primitive form previously, is attributed to the Huns in the fifth and sixth centuries AD.

A proper saddle and stirrups allowed for far greater control over the horse. It made mounting easier, and also allowed for a better performance from the horse, as it is able to go further and faster if the rider can stand up in the saddle and lean forward at a gallop. Even slower paces, a trot for example, can be sustained longer if the rider receives some support from stirrups and the fact that this in turn means he is not bumping about awkwardly on the horse's back makes it far less tiring for the animal too.

Throughout the early centuries AD at least up until the Middle Ages, riding was mostly confined to warfare. Some people would have travelled on horseback but this would almost always have been out of necessity, not for pleasure. Probably the only recreational use of the horse was in hunting and other such sporting pursuits.

As the techniques of warfare became a little more sophisticated and efficient, the horse's role altered somewhat, although it was many centuries before it was no longer needed. Towards the end of the Middle Ages, developments in weaponry meant the heavily armoured knight no longer had a place on the battlefield, and the tournaments and jousts that had hitherto been serious battle training became merely spectacles of pageantry and ceremony. Classical equitation became an art rather than an active part of the training of the war horse, although it was still mainly practised by the cavalry rather than civilians.

The sixteenth century onward saw the rise of the great European riding schools, and these were the heart of classical equitation or *haute école*. The

most famous of all must be the Spanish Riding School of Vienna, begun in 1572 in order to train the Spanish horses of the Archduke. It was not until some time later that the school became renowned for the beautiful white Lipizzaner stallions that are still trained there today.

Haute école equitation involves the training of horse and rider in advanced paces and movements that are known as the 'airs on the ground' and the 'airs above the ground'. The airs on the ground are the *piaffe, passage* and *pirouette*. The *piaffe* is an elevated trot (that is, the legs being lifted considerably higher than usual) performed on the spot, while the *passage*, known sometimes as the Spanish trot, is an elevated trot in which the horse moves slowly forward to give the impression of almost floating over the ground. A *pirouette* is an extremely advanced movement usually performed at a canter in which the horse turns either through 180 degrees or 360 degrees in the length of its own body, so that it effectively pivots on its inner hindleg.

In the airs above the ground, the horse either lifts its front legs off the ground or actually springs off the ground with all four legs. The best known and most spectacular movements are the *levade*, the *courbette* and the *capriole*. In the *levade*, the horse lifts its forehand in the air while crouching back on sharply bent hocks. The forelegs are bent close in to the chest. In the *courbette*, the animal assumes the same position as in the *levade* and then springs forward from its hocks in a series of short jumps, its forelegs never touching the ground. This requires immense strength in the hock joints, and it is this strength that determines the number of jumps forward a horse is able to make in the movement. The magnificent *capriole* is a single leap into the air in which the forelegs are bent beneath the horse's body and the hind legs are stretched out behind so that the shoes are visible.

Equitation at this level of expertise is achieved by only a few horses and riders, but riding for pleasure and recreation is widely practised throughout the world

Left: *There are few more pleasant pastimes for the horse-lover than a hack through the countryside on a sunny day.* (Peter Roberts)

Below left: *Riders can indulge their hobby in the very heart of a busy metropolis. Here they are riding through Hyde Park, situated in the centre of London.* (British Tourist Association)

Below: *A covered school or menage is the best place to school a young horse or pony or to receive instruction in riding technique.* (Peter Roberts/C. A. Visual)

nowadays. In the past few decades especially, the role of the horse has shifted from helping man with his daily work to helping him to enjoy his leisure time.

It is easy to understand the attractions of riding: it may be practised by almost anybody, whatever their age, the only real criterion being whether they are able to hoist themselves up into the saddle! It is possible to ride in almost any country of the world, in both urban and rural areas — even in large metropolitan cities, if there are parks where riding is permitted or specially constructed riding ménages. It can be a solitary or social pastime and is undoubtedly a way of escaping for a time the rush and bustle of modern life, with the added satisfaction of establishing an understanding with another living creature.

There are many, many different types of riding horse and pony. Some are more suited to different terrains and habitats than others; some are bred for a specific type of riding, such as hunting or showing, racing or eventing. Different nationalities favour different breeds and most countries have developed their own local types or breeds of riding horse.

As discussed in the last chapter, there are nine native pony breeds in the British Isles, all of which make excellent children's riding ponies when broken in to the saddle. When brought into such domestic situations, these native ponies generally become family pets, and will be handed down to younger brothers and sisters. Many a rider has begun his or her riding career on a Shetland pony (as the famous cartoonist Thelwell bears witness) and many a tear has been shed when the pony is outgrown by the child!

The most famous riding horse to have been created in Great Britain and possibly in the world is the Thoroughbred. Nowadays it will be found in many different branches of horsemanship, but

it was originally developed specifically for racing. The Thoroughbred was first recognized as a breed in the late eighteenth and early nineteenth centuries and owes its origin to three Arabian stallions imported into the country at that time. All pure British Thoroughbreds can trace their pedigree back to one of these horses. Thoroughbreds are now bred all over the world and many countries have their own breed of Thoroughbred.

The Arabian itself is one of the most beautiful riding horses of all and is responsible for influencing and helping to produce countless other breeds the world over. Originating centuries ago in Arabia, it is now bred in many different countries which have developed their own recognized strains.

The offspring of an Arabian crossed with a Thoroughbred is known as an Anglo-Arab and is a recognized breed. It has been developed mainly in Great Britain, France and Poland and is an elegant, lightweight saddle horse. It is a good all-round riding horse, although probably a little too refined to be kept as a general purpose, utility family animal. Many successful show hacks have been Anglo-Arabs, while this breed has also done well in the competitive worlds of dressage, eventing and jumping.

In a number of European countries, horse breeding is state controlled and all stallions are kept at national studs. This means that the bloodlines of all breeds and types of horse can be kept pure and also allows new breeds to be developed with discretion. In France, all horse breeding is under the control of the government and the French produce some excellent riding horses. In comparatively recent years, they have produced a saddle horse known as the French Saddle Horse or the Selle Française. It is a very handsome animal, standing about 15.2 to 16.3 hands high and has had great success in eventing and show jumping. This breed was produced by crossing local mares with Arabs and Thoroughbreds, so there are slight regional variations. All, however, make excellent riding horses.

The Swedish government was also instrumental in creating a national riding horse that has excelled in the competitive fields of dressage and jumping. This is the Swedish Half-Bred, which stands about the same height at the French Saddle Horse. It was developed by crossing Thoroughbreds and German horses with local mares. Now a recognized breed is fixed and a national stud has been established at Flyinge in southern Sweden. Here, three-year old stallions are subjected to a series of rigorous speed, soundness and temperament tests and are only allowed to breed if they pass all of them at the required standard. As a result, the Swedish Half-Bred is a magnificent saddle horse, renowned for its equable, intelligent temperament and athletic movement.

Germany has several excellent riding horse breeds, which differ very little in

Below: The famous cartoonist, Thelwell, has brought amusement to millions with his accurate portrayal of young riders and their Shetland-type ponies. (Punch/Peter Roberts)

Right: Sometimes it is not difficult to see where the maestro finds his subjects! (Peter Roberts)

Below right: The beautiful head of a Thoroughbred foal — among the nearest perfect of all horse breeds. (Peter Roberts)

appearance and performance. Among them are the Holstein, the Hanoverian, the Württemberg, the Bavarian Warm Blood, the Oldenburg and the Trakehner. All stand on average about 16 hands high and are riding horses of considerable quality. Some of these breeds have been in existence in Germany since the seventeenth century, but have been 'improved' in recent years by infusions of Thoroughbred and other blood. This is tending to iron out some of the different features and characteristics of the various breeds, so that a standard type of German Riding Horse is beginning to emerge.

Besides the Mustang discussed in the last chapter, the United States of America has some excellent saddle horses, all of which have been developed during the last two hundred years. The oldest breed is the Quarter Horse, known internationally for its versatility. Its name derives from the fact that the early settlers used to race their horses over short distances of about a quarter of a mile, often along the town's main — or only — street. Nowadays, special racing Quarter Horses are bred and are said to

Above: *Another beautiful head — this time of an Arabian. The characteristic neat, pricked ears, 'dished' nose or concave facial profile and large flaring nostrils are well illustrated here.* (Peter Roberts)

Right: *A fine example of the French Saddle Horse or* Selle Française — *a superb riding horse noted for its courage and pleasant temperament.* (ARDEA)

be the fastest in the world over this distance. The breed is also immensely popular in all aspects of western riding and its apparently natural instinct for working cattle makes it a favourite mount of cowboys on the ranch and at the rodeo.

The Morgan is another of America's oldest breeds of saddle horse. It took its name from the foundation stallion of the breed which belonged to a schoolteacher called Justin Morgan. Morgans have played an important part in establishing the other American breeds, such as the Tennessee Walking Horse, and the American Saddlebred and Standardbred. The Tennessee Walking Horse has a unique running walk, performed by no other breed but extremely comfortable for the rider. The American Saddlebred has unusual movement too, in that besides the conventional paces of walk, trot and canter, it also moves at a 'slow gait' and a 'rack'. The rack is a four-beat pace which produces a spectacular, prancing movement, while the slow gait is the same basic pace, but performed much slower so that it is extremely graceful to watch. The American Standardbred is a harness racing horse, not a saddle horse.

There are scores of other breeds of riding horse the world over, far too numerous to mention here; one more, however, is worthy of inclusion by virtue of its unusual gait. This is the Paso. There are various types of this breed, but all possess the unique gait, known also as the Paso. It is a four-beat gait in which the forelegs are lifted in what appears to be an exaggerated outward swing while the hind legs move in a straight line taking very long, direct strides. Although it is a four-beat pace, each lateral pair of legs moves forward at almost the same time.

Of the many, many millions of people who ride, probably only a comparatively

Right: *The characteristic high-stepping gait of the Paso breeds of horse may be seen here. Note, too, the ornate harness and unusual 'box' stirrups — trappings for the show ring.* (ZEFA)

Below: *A lovely painting of an American Quarter Horse, one of the most popular breeds in the US.* (Peter Roberts)

small percentage own their own horses or ponies. Circumstances often make it impossible to do so and for the casual weekend rider, riding schools provide an excellent service. The standard of riding schools varies greatly, however, some using old, tired, bored or broken-down horses made unresponsive through years of bad riding and handling. It is as well, therefore, to check out a few riding schools before deciding on the one that will get your custom.

For those people that do have their own horse or pony, there are a number of possible ways of keeping it. Which is most suitable will depend on individual circumstances as well as on the type of animal involved. Most family or children's riding ponies, except for valuable show animals, can be kept out at grass all year round. The field in which they are kept should provide adequate grazing (although this will usually have to be supplemented with hay, and sometimes solid feed as well, in the winter), have a constant supply of fresh water and be surrounded by good fencing with a strong gate. It is preferable to provide some sort of shelter too, such as a three-sided shed, to give protection against bad weather in the winter and bothersome flies in the summer.

Better bred horses, such as Thorough-

Right: *Horses will often lie down and roll when turned out in a field, particularly after a long, hot ride.* (Peter Roberts)

Below: *Dutch horses grazing beside a dyke in their native Holland.* (Peter Roberts)

breds or those used for competition work or hunting, will usually be stabled, at least during the winter or the time of the year they are in work. The care of such an animal is far more time-consuming than that of a horse or pony kept out at grass; they need regular feeding (a stabled horse usually receives four feeds a day), and thorough daily grooming and exercise to keep them healthy and fit.

Some people keep horses and ponies on a combined system — turning them out during the day and bringing them in at night or vice versa. This has the advantage that the animals can exercise themselves naturally in the field and yet are a little fitter and easier to keep looking respectable than one that is turned out all the time. And for those who lead busy town and office lives but still want to have their own horse or pony, the livery stable, where the animal's care and welfare is in the hands of paid grooms, can provide the perfect answer.

Right: *Grooming time in the yard of a busy livery stable situated on the outskirts of a big city.* (Peter Roberts)

Below: *Stable chores can seem endless when looking after a stabled animal. Mucking-out is one of the 'delights' that must be done every day.* (Peter Roberts)

The Working Horse

Pages 48 & 49: *Horses still help a farmer in Buholz, Austria to cut the grass in his orchard.* (ZEFA)

Below: *The use of horses as agricultural workers is not totally a thing of the past. Here a farmer in the Black Forest, Germany employs equine power to help him till the land.* (Peter Roberts)

In the last chapter, the changing role of the horse in man's life was discussed. Yet this difference between being a 'work' animal and one used for recreational pastimes is probably a distinction that has escaped the horse! Whether harnessed between the shafts of a plough or ridden quietly through a pleasant grove, it is doubtless all work to the horse. However, it is possible for our purposes to differentiate between these two ways in which the horse is used by man.

One of the most common visions of horses at work must surely be that of the magnificent heavy horses employed all over the world until comparatively recent times in farm work. In fact horses were first used in this way rather later in history than one might imagine, for in earlier times it was oxen, or very often, women who were used to pull the ploughs and other implements of cultivation. If a farmer owned a horse, he generally saved it for more important tasks, such as taking him and his wife

into town on market days. When horses began to be used on the farm their jobs were manifold, from ploughing and harrowing the land in preparation for sowing, to helping to reap the harvest and bringing in the loaded hay carts and wagons. In addition, they were frequently used to drive static farm machinery, such as threshing machines, corn mills and butter churns. To do this, they were harnessed to a shaft and made to walk round in endless circles, turning the cogs on the crude mechanism.

The horses most commonly associated with farm work are the massive heavy or cart-horses, although in fact horses of all types have been used through the ages in varying parts of the world. In those places where heavy horses have not been bred, farmers had to make use of the local animals at their disposal. In Iceland, for example, it is the little Icelandic ponies that have always been the agricultural workers and indeed they still are in many regions.

British heavy horses are among the

Below: *A horse is driven endlessly round a wooden post to help thresh the corn in Greece.* (ZEFA)

best known in the world and include the Suffolk Punch, the Clydesdale and the Shire, which originated in East Anglia, Lanarkshire and the midland Shire counties respectively. The Suffolk Punch, which is always chestnut-coloured, although it can be any one of seven different shades, is considered to be one of the purest of all breeds of heavy horse. The Clydesdale was developed during the eighteenth century to meet the need for a strong animal to haul heavy loads and is usually bay, brown or black, while the stately Shire with its distinctive white feather is said to be descended from the 'Great Horse' that carried the armoured knights of the Middle Ages.

As mechanization took over as the most efficient way to undertake farm work, the future of these superb breeds looked somewhat bleak and their numbers decreased dramatically. More recently, however, there has been a considerable revival of interest in the heavy horse breeds as a whole and societies have been formed to protect them. They are frequently seen at horse

shows, in displays or parades, and many rural areas hold ploughing competitions in which carthorses provide the tractive power. In some places, too, they will still be seen at work on the land, although the most common work use to which they are put nowadays is to pull brewers' drays as they deliver their beer barrels to town and city pubs. The breweries that employ heavy horses in this way maintain that it is not just an advertising gimmick, but in localized areas around the brewery it is actually the most economical and convenient way of making deliveries.

Of the other breeds of heavy horse in the world, the French Percheron is one of the best known. This huge but characteristically docile animal is bred in many different countries and is perhaps the most popular carthorse of all. France has a number of other heavy horse breeds, such as the Boulonnais, Breton and Ardennais, the last of which also comes from Belgium. All have been employed in agricultural work or rural activities of some sort through the ages and many can still be seen working on

Above: *A farmer in Iceland uses a pony and cart in a remote area to save the aching legs of the younger members of the family.* (Solarfilma)

Right: *Britain's famous heavy horses are nowadays most frequently seen in action between the shafts at regional plough-ing contests.* (Police Federation)

Left: Magnificent Shire horses are put to use at the Horse of the Year Show in London to gently harrow the surface of the indoor arena ready for the next event. (Peter Roberts)

Below: Horses are used to pull the loaded drays of breweries in many countries. These ones are pictured in Lucerne, Switzerland. (Peter Roberts)

the land in isolated areas. In the wine areas of France, for example, horses are often used to help bring in the grapes at harvesting time.

Although it would not perhaps be quite accurate to describe them as 'agricultural' workers, horses play a vital and active role in farm or ranch life in Canada, the United States of America, and Australia. To the cowboys who work the cattle that is the life blood of such establishments, horses are of immense importance and a good 'cow' horse is worth its weight in gold. They are trained in herding cattle so that they know what to do instinctively, singling out a particular animal from the herd at

the merest indication from the rider and throwing their weight against a bucking steer which has just been roped by the cowboy. In other parts of the world where herds of cattle are turned out to graze on vast expanses of fenceless plains or prairies, such as in Hungary, horses are used in a similar way, and in the Camargue area of France the *gardiens* use them in their daily work (see page 27) as they patrol and check the marshes.

As a haulage animal, the horse has been used in a myriad ways since time immemorial. In the ancient world it pulled the chariots of the leaders and heroes; it helped the early settlers in the United States of America in their

56

Below: *The horse here is an Appaloosa whose ancestry may be traced back to the Nez Perce Indians.* (Peter Roberts)

Right: *A cowboy in Red Lodge Montana quietly herds the cattle on the range.* (US Travel Service)

westward trek across the Continent by drawing the huge covered wagons that held all their belongings; it pulled the coaches and carriages of the nobility of all Europe for countless generations, just as it will still be seen between the shafts of the British Royal carriages on state occasions today. In all major cities in the world from New York to London to Peking, before the invention of the internal combustion engine it pulled the dust carts, the furniture wagons, the ambulances, the stage and mail coaches, the milk floats, the elegant cabs, the omnibuses and trams — even the funeral hearses. All the tradesmen — the butcher, the baker, the coal man, the greengrocer — did their daily rounds in horse-drawn vehicles of one type or another. Such services have no part in modern life however, and almost the only horse-drawn carriages to be seen in major towns and cities today are those used as tourist attractions to take visitors on conducted tours of places of historic interest. Occasionally too, in London, the 'rag-and-bone' man may still be seen, and heard, travelling around the streets with his junk-laden open cart, usually pulled by a rough little pony that looks as if it has seen better days.

Among the most famous of all American work horses must surely be those that operated the Pony Express from the spring of 1860 to the autumn of 1861. This service carried the mail over a distance of 2900 kilometres (1800 miles) between Missouri and California. The journey was scheduled to take ten days and involved some twenty-four riders mounted on Quarter Horses (see page 40). Merciless weather conditions that often washed away tracks and blocked passes with heavy snow drifts, together with the hostile Indians and marauding outlaws, made it a hazardous job for the riders and the mail rarely reached its destination on time. These

Left: *Horses still pull the coaches of the British Royal family on many occasions. Here, Queen Elizabeth the Queen Mother parades around the famous Ascot race-course.* (Peter Roberts)

Below: *Not too much business on a snowy day for these horse-drawn sleighs, waiting to show tourists the sights of Zermatt.* (Peter Roberts)

dangers, combined with the advent of the telegraph line, which was completed in October 1861, brought the service to an end.

Nor was it only in the United States of America that the postal system relied upon the use of horses. Throughout Eurasia, particularly in those places where there were no inland waterways or canals which allowed the transport of mail on the barges (many of which were horse-drawn anyway), the horse was the only means of communication between towns and villages. In Victorian Britain the mail coaches, which also carried passengers, adhered to a timetable that would put the public transport system of today to shame!

In the world of entertainment, the horse has also played an important role. The movie industry and cinema box-offices the world over owe much to equine super-stars. In Western movies in particular, horses like Champion and Trigger are remembered as dearly as their riders. The training of such horses is incredibly exacting and a horse in a leading role will be put through a training programme that may last many months. During this time, like any actor, it is taught the rudiments of conduct in front of the camera. For a horse, these include walking towards the camera, stopping at any prescribed spot,

Above: *The mail coach was a familiar sight in Victorian Britain.* (Mary Evans Picture Library)

Right: *Horses have been the super-stars of many a big screen movie. Showy palaminos, such as this one, dressed in wildly ornate and glittering harness, make a spectacular picture.* (ZEFA)

Below: *Work horses of all types have been depicted on postage stamps in countries the world over.* (Peter Roberts)

stepping backwards, looking to left, right or behind, limping, feigning pain, rearing, pawing the ground, shaking its head, falling with a rider and lying down pretending to be dead — all performed instantly at an off-screen cue from the trainer.

The circus is another area in the world of entertainment where horses still give immense pleasure to huge numbers of spectators in many different countries. Again the training of a circus horse is a lengthy and delicate business, for a foot wrong in the middle of a split-second timed bareback stunt could mean death to a rider. Circus horses perform in the tiny ring with and without riders. Some are trained to canter rhythmically round and round, never altering speed or breaking pace, while the riders perform their breathtaking balancing acts. In other instances, beautiful liberty horses are put through their highly-polished routines — sometimes ridden, sometimes directed from the trainer on the ground — but always moving in perfect harmony and unison.

One of the worst jobs ponies have ever been called upon to do was working in the coal mines. Until ten to fifteen years ago small ponies, Shetlands in particular, would spend most of their lives as 'pit ponies' underground, pulling the coal-laden wagons from the coal seams to the mine shafts. In the early days of coal-mining, the ponies led miserable lives, living in perpetual subterranean gloom which sent many of them blind. More recently, however, the Coal Mines Act laid down certain rules and regulations about the treatment of the ponies and the conditions in which they should live, which considerably improved their working lives. The old 'tubs' they were once made to haul full of coal were replaced by lighter trucks; their stables were ventilated by fresh air ducts and the food fed to them was protected from dust, which amazingly had not been the case hitherto. When their days in the pits were over, they were retired to the pleasant pastures of special 'homes of rest' where it was assured they would never work again.

If Shetland and other small ponies are

no longer called upon to work in the coal mines, a new job has emerged for the native or cross-breed type of ponies in recent years and one that is of immense value. This is the role they play in the programme known as Riding for the Disabled — an idea which originated in Norway and happily has spread to a number of other countries. It was discovered that teaching handicapped people to ride was good exercise and immensely therapeutic as well as bringing them enormous enjoyment. Many aids, such as specially constructed saddles, are used and the ponies are given special training so that their reliability is beyond doubt.

It is perhaps a little ironic that one of the most significant ways this most peaceable of animals has been of service to man is in helping him to fight his wars and battles. Horses were first used to draw chariots into war well over a thousand years before Christ and mounted warriors first wrought death and destruction among their enemies in 900 BC. From then on, right up until the Second World War, horses have often played a leading role in man's seemingly endless battles.

Besides being the moving force of a ridden cavalry charge, horses have pulled vehicles of war the world over — from the heavy wheel-mounted guns and canons to the ambulances and medical supplies wagons. The mounted scout was of vital importance to an army, as astride his fast, nimble pony he could discover the whereabouts of the enemy with little danger of being detected.

Distasteful though such a use of the horse might seem, its training for war through the ages is responsible for many of the active pursuits of the equestrian fraternity today. As we have seen in previous chapters, the movements of *haute école* and *dressage* practised today were first taught as disciplinary and

Previous page: *Equine performances at a circus are always popular. Here a line-up of brightly-plumed liberty horses prepare to take their final bow.* (Peter Roberts)

Right: *One of the most famous army generals of all, Napoleon, had many favourite horses. This magnificent statue stands permanent sentinel at Leffrey, near Grenoble.* (Peter Roberts)

Below: *Ponies are no longer put to work in the coal mines of Britain, but occasionally they are brought out on parade at a show as reminders of less happy times past.* (Peter Roberts)

Above: *Members of the Argentinian mounted guard march in formation along a street in Buenos Aires.* (ZEFA)

Left: *Members of the King's Troop of the Royal Horse Artillery on the parade ground. It takes seven horses, three of them mounted, to pull the heavy gun carriages.* (Peter Roberts)

tactical movements for the battlefields. Many equestrian sports — eventing, hunting, even polo — owe much to the initiative and patronage of mounted army officers.

Most countries of the world still have mounted troops, although their main duties now are to attend ceremonial occasions. In London, the resplendent officers of such troops as the Household Cavalry, The Royal Regiment of the Blues and the King's Troop of the Royal Cavalry, mounted on their magnificently cared-for and immaculately turned-out horses are a popular sight, whether out on exercise, or attending the Royal carriages on state occasions.

The other important role played by the horse in maintaining law and order is that of the mounted police forces. Again, police horses are a common sight moving in stately fashion along the roads of most major cities in the world — from Tehran, where the police ride spirited stallions that are nevertheless trained to stand absolutely motionless while a rifle is fired from their backs, to Barcelona where the police control the unruly crowds from stately Andalusians. In

Tokyo and in the capital cities of Australia, street crossings are often controlled by mounted police.

The most famous mounted police force of all must be the Royal Canadian Mounties. Established at the end of the nineteenth century, when they were known as the North-West Mounted Police, their job was to keep the peace between the Indians who had lived in this huge, ungoverned area for generations, and the foreign traders and settlers whom the Indians saw as a perpetual threat to their land, their stock and their livelihood. The scarlet-coated figures of the Mounties became undisputed symbols of law and justice, striking fear in the hearts of criminals who knew that the Mounties 'always get their man', but representing comfort and security to all law-abiding citizens. Today the famous black horses which have long been associated with the Mounties are still bred and trained at Fort Walsh, although the Force is really no longer operational in upholding the law. Instead they undertake a role of almost equal importance as ambassadors, touring the world to give their famous displays of riding to music.

Australia had at one time a similar police force, whose job was to patrol the vast uncharted outback where the lives of the early homesteaders, struggling to establish a living in the face of tremendous natural adversity, were further threatened by the notorious outback outlaws — such as Ned Kelly and his murderous gang. This police force was known as the Trooper police and again is no longer active in law enforcement.

The work demanded and expected of police horses the world over is very similar and the horses that become the mounts of policemen are often very similar in type — sensible, strong horses, with good breeding, an equable temperament and considerable intelligence. The breeds used vary, however, according to location and availability and there is no particular breed of police horse. Those used in England are generally cross-breeds, probably with some Thoroughbred in their lineage.

Previous page: *The famous red-coated Mounties from Canada performing their musical ride.* (Peter Roberts)

Left: *A police horse walks quietly along the road by the side of an ordered crowd in an English town.* (Police Federation)

Below: *Queen Elizabeth II rides a police horse at the annual Trooping of the Colour.* (Peter Roberts)

The training of police horses is undertaken with patient routine, often by the officers who will eventually care for and ride the animals. They are taught the techniques of crowd control, how to stand still and firm, pitting their weight against an angry throng of shouting people. They must be trained to ignore all unpleasant and noisy distractions — bangs, shouts, drum beats, waving banners, hurled missiles of varying natures, even umbrellas being opened in their faces or newspapers waved under their noses. And they must remain calm under any circumstances; a mounted policeman must know that even if his horse is brought to its knees, perhaps by marbles being thrown under its feet or somebody tripping it up, it will not panic. That the British monarch always rides a police horse at the annual Trooping the Colour, during which the mount must behave impeccably and stand still for hours on end, is an indication of the thoroughness of their training and a measure of their reliability.

Of the many ways in which the horse has worked, and continues to work, for mankind, the role of the police horse must be one of the most exacting of all, and it is perhaps one of the few that is as important today as it has ever been.

The Competition Horse

Above: *Ancient chariot races were the forerunners of today's harness racing. Happily current rules make for rather less of a free-for-all!* (Mansell Collection)

Right: *Trotters race round a cinder track. If a horse breaks out of a trot during a race, it is not penalized, but loses valuable time as it is pulled back to the trotting pace.* (ZEFA)

Pages 72 & 73: *Britain's David Broome on Sportsman takes a fence in his usual quiet, impeccable style. The fence comprises a balustrade topped by a couple of white-painted poles.* (Peter Roberts)

For over 2000 years, man's competitive instinct has led him to set horses against one another in competition. At one time, equestrian competitions were entirely amateur affairs, the purpose being only to establish which person or which horse was the 'best'. Nowadays most competitive equestrianism has a professional side, and huge sums of money are invested in it.

The oldest of all competitive horse sports, and the one that is now the biggest business, is racing. It is easy to imagine that from the very beginnings of horse-riding, testing the speed of one horse against another would be a simple and indisputable way of proving supremacy.

Harness racing, now less popular than mounted racing, is in fact the oldest of all equestrian sports and began with the chariot races of the early Roman, Greek and Egyptian civilizations. Nowadays, harness racing is most popular in the United States of America, Canada, Australia, New Zealand and Russia as well as in various European countries such as France, Germany, Norway and

Sweden. The sport falls into two main categories, according to the horses' gait: trotting and pacing. Trotting horses race at a conventional, but extended and very fast, trotting pace — that is, diagonal front and hind legs moving together. The legs of a pacer move laterally — that is, the front and hind legs on one side move forwards together. In both cases, they pull a light, two-wheeled carriage or sulky in which the driving 'jockey' is seated.

It would be fair to say that the United States of America leads the world in harness racing and its racehorse, the Standardbred, is popular for both forms of harness racing in many countries. The name of the breed is derived from the 'standard' time in which it must cover a 1.8 kilometre (1 mile) distance.

Russia has a famous trotting breed in the Orlov Trotter, developed at the end of the eighteenth and beginning of the nineteenth centuries by Count Alexei Orlov. Trotting races are extremely popular in Russia and there are more than thirty state studs breeding trotting horses. France and Germany have also

both developed their own breed of trotting horse, the German Trotter owing much to the Orlov Trotter, which was its main ancestor. The French Trotter was developed by crossing their all-purpose Norman horses with Thoroughbreds. It is rather bigger than most other trotting breeds because some French trotting races are ridden, which demands a stronger horse.

Organized mounted racing, as opposed to friendly challenges between individuals, is documented as first taking place at the 624 BC Olympiad. Since then its passage through history has been chequered, sometimes favoured, sometimes falling into great disrepute, so that it is alternately known as the Sport of Kings or the Pastime of the Devil! Nowadays it is firmly established as a major sport all over the world and literally thousands of people are employed in the business, at many levels, as well as countless others who follow its progress either at the race tracks of the world or on television.

Racing falls into two main categories — that conducted on the 'flat' and that practised over jumps, known as steeplechasing or hurdling. Flat racing is the oldest of these and the one involving both the most professionalism and the most money. In Great Britain, the most famous races are the Epsom Derby, the St Leger, the Oaks and the Thousand and Two Thousand Guineas, all of which have been run since the end of the eighteenth century or the beginning of the nineteenth century.

In America, most flat races are run on 'dirt' tracks as opposed to the grass or 'turf' of British courses. It was in the States too, that mechanized starting stalls, now a familiar sight on race tracks the world over, originated. America's most famous flat races are the Kentucky Derby, the Belmont Stakes and the Preakness Stakes first run in 1875, 1867 and 1873 respectively. Furthermore, it was an American jockey who was responsible for the crouched racing seat which all jockeys use today. Called Tod Sloan, he discovered that a horse could gallop faster if the jockey rode crouching forward up the horse's neck with very short stirrup leathers, rather than sitting in the conventional 'hunting-seat' position.

Racing over fences had its beginning in eighteenth century England when country squires tested their horses' speed against one another across country, jumping the fences, hedges and ditches in their path. The first races were run

Above: *An old sporting print of Ascot Heath races in 1837, twenty-six years after the course was opened at the instigation of Queen Anne.* (Mansell Collection)

Right: *Ascot races today. The crowd now cheer from the shelter of the grandstand.* (Peter Roberts)

from the steeple on one village church to that of a neighbouring village — hence the name steeplechasing. This form of racing is most popular in Ireland and Great Britain, and the notorious British Grand National is the most famous steeplechase of all. France has some famous steeplechase races, too, of which the Grand Steeplechase de Paris is the equivalent of the Grand National. Steeplechases and hurdle races are held in the United States of America, both featuring obstacles constructed of soft brush. In addition, racing is also conducted over courses of rather more formidable fixed post and rail fences.

In all forms of racing, but flat racing in particular, it is the Thoroughbred that is the competition horse. This is the breed that was created in Great Britain at the beginning of the eighteenth century specifically for this sport (see page 37).

The competitive worlds of show jumping and eventing are younger than racing, but with the advent of television they have gained immensely in popularity as spectator sports over the last couple of decades. Show jumping is the practice of jumping over a series or 'course' of man-made jumps arranged in a specific order in a confined space. Eventing is divided into three main phases — a *dressage* test, a fairly lengthy ride over a cross-country course of 'natural' obstacles (often still man-made but natural in that they comprise hedges, ditches and jumps constructed from wooden posts and rails or tree trunks and branches), and a show jumping phase.

The origins of show-jumping and when it first became an organized competitive sport are somewhat obscure. The first competitions were known as 'leaping' contests and some appear to have been held in the mid- to late nineteenth century. However, it was not until the beginning of the twentieth century that they began to be held more regularly. Show jumping competitions in these early days were not particularly interesting to ride or watch; most courses consisted of from two to six upright fences of unpainted poles placed in a

Horse racing in the US is mainly conducted on dirt tracks. The mobile starting stalls can be seen to the back of the picture. (ZEFA)

straight line on either side of an arena with perhaps a simple spread jump in the centre. The rider merely rode around the ring, jumping all the jumps in sequence before turning down the middle. Besides taking as long as he wanted to complete the course, there were no penalties for circling in front of the fence (which constitutes a refusal under today's rules), or even for getting off to make some adjustment to the saddlery in between jumps. Judging was complicated, and by no means standardised internationally, and it could take considerable time and discussion to agree upon the score for a round. Happily, the formation of the *Fédération Equestre Internationale* in 1921 did much to iron out at least some of the inconsistencies in the sport's regulations.

Between the Wold Wars, show jumping courses began to be improved, although they still consisted mainly of upright fences. Many countries were now participating in the sport interna-

tionally, but in the 1930s, its popularity waned in Great Britain, while it thrived in the rest of Europe. Continental competitions were more exciting for riders and spectators as their rules imposed a time limit for completing the course in most major events, a regulation not included in the British rules at the time. This gave riders in other parts of Europe the advantage of learning to take their fences at speed even in a confined space.

After World War II, show jumping in Britain took on a very different style. Thanks to the vision of some British officers, who during their time as prisoners-of-war planned the shape of show jumping in the future, some dramatic changes took place. Realizing the importance of injecting some interest into the sport, they introduced courses of mixed fences — that is, some upright jumps, some spreads, and some combinations (two or three fences positioned with only a stride or two in

Above: *Many of the early steeplechases were madcap races conducted across country by moonlight.* (Mansell Collection)

Right: *A modern show jumping course. A variety of brightly painted 'artificial' fences are packed into an amazingly small indoor arena.* (Peter Roberts)

Left: *Harvey Smith is among the most controversial, as well as repeatedly successful, of all show jumping personalities.* (Peter Roberts)

Above: *In spite of the seemingly impossible angle, David Broome and Beethoven did clear this water jump.* (Joyce Pope)

between), all made of colourfully painted poles and with bright pots of flowers placed on the ground in front of them. Sceptical riders had to approve this revolution when they found their horses jumped the fences willingly, accurately and with greater boldness.

Top level show jumping today is a truly international sport and riders of all nationalities will be seen regularly at the major shows of the world. These include the National Horse Show at Madison Square Garden in New York, the Toronto Winter Fair in Canada, the Aachen Show in Germany, the Royal International and Horse of the Year Show in London and others of equal fame in Nice, Rome, Madrid, Dublin, Lucerne and Rotterdam.

There is no particular breed of show jumper and those seen in the international rings vary considerably in shape,

Left: *German riders are among the leaders in international show jumping: here Karl Huck rides Alvaro.* (Peter Roberts)

Below: *One of the most famous show jumpers of all, Bill Steinkraus from the US.* (Joyce Pope)

Overleaf: *This arid show jumping ring in Victoria, Australia contrasts sharply the greener European rings.* (ZEFA)

size, colour and breeding. However, they are all horses that have a unique athletic ability and talent for jumping, for it is not 'natural' for a horse to be able to jump the enormous heights and widths of international show jumping fences.

Similarly, there is no recognized breed of eventer, but in this sport almost more than any other an animal is required that displays great courage, obedience, versatility and general all-round talent, for it has to excel in three quite different fields of equestrianism. Although, like show-jumping, eventing has become increasingly popular in comparatively recent times, its origins go back a long way, in fact once again to the training of horses in military riding academies.

Understandably the first eventing competitions, which were held at the beginning of the twentieth century, were completely dominated by the military, but after World War II, more and more civilians began to take part. Initially, eventing found most support on the European mainland but in the late 1940s and early 1950s, British riders began to be more and more active in the sport. One of the most famous three-day events in the world is now held annually in Badminton Park in Gloucester. Eventing is supported today by all the riding nations of the world.

Because eventing comprises three phases, major eventing competitions are always held over three days. Day one is a

Above: *Eventing was once considered too physically demanding for women riders; however Lorna Sutherland and many others have had repeated successes in top class events.* (Peter Roberts)

Right: *The Royal patronage of Princess Anne and her husband Mark Phillips, seen here on Great Ovation, has done much to increase the sport's popularity.* (Peter Roberts)

dressage test, where a high level of skill is called for, although it is not a difficult test by international *dressage* standards. Day two is the most testing day of all and generally begins with a course of roads and tracks. This is followed by a steeple-chase course, which includes a dozen or so racing fences. Then there is another course over roads and tracks, before the supreme test — the cross-country.

This is the part of the competition that draws the crowds, for unlike the jumps in a show-jumping ring, the fences are fixed and solid. Thirty to thirty-five fences are laid out over a course of about 8 kilometres (5 miles)

and include obstacles in and out of lakes, combination fences, high piles of logs, banks, hedges and ditches and anything else the course builders can devise!

On the final day, providing the horse has successfully passed a veterinary examination, it participates in a show jumping event. Small perhaps by top international standards, the course is still sufficiently big and demanding to test the horse's skill and fitness.

Among the most graceful of all competitive equestrianism is the art of *dressage* which is the supreme test of suppleness, lightness and precision

Above: *A top-class competitor performing an intricate dressage movement.* (Peter Roberts)

Left: *Italy's Anna Casagrande and Daleye make light work of one of the more formidable obstacles at the Badminton Horse Trials.* (Peter Roberts)

Pages 87: *M. Thomas sits well back over a steeplechase type fence.* (Peter Roberts)

obedience in a horse. It attracts less spectators than other competitive events, perhaps because to enjoy it requires greater understanding and knowledge of the paces and movements performed. It has its origins in the classical equitation of the great riding schools.

Competition dressage involves a number of tests in which the type and sequence of movement is specified and defined. At the highest levels these tests are the Prix St Georges, the Grand Prix and the Olympic Tests and they include some of the airs on the ground (see page 36) such as the *passage* and *piaffe*. The airs above the ground, however, belong strictly to the art of *haute école*.

Although international competition dressage is spreading its net wider and more countries are beginning to compete, it is European riders, Germany in particular, that have long led the field. Whereas most countries have had no more than a handful of horses and riders at Grand Prix level, Germany has been able to produce hundreds.

Again, there is no specific breed of dressage horse and different countries favour different breeds. American and British riders like the fine, Thoroughbred-type animals, while riders from other countries tend to use their own particular native-bred animals which are often of heavier build.

The training of a top level dressage horse is an extremely lengthy business and very few horses possess all the qualities necessary to take them to the top. It is said to take at least six years to train a horse to world-class level, which perhaps also helps to explain why this remains one of the most specialized branches of equestrian competition.

The world of competitive showing is another that has perhaps fewer followers than the more spectacular, easier to understand competitive events. And yet at one time it was the showing classes that were the main, if not the only, events at a horse show. Although in some classes, show horses are judged partly on performance, it is really the conformation and turn-out of the animal that most affects the judging.

Show classes vary tremendously across the world. In Great Britain, there are classes for hunters of many different types (a 'hunter' is a horse considered suitable to follow hounds, although in fact few show hunters ever see the hunting field); there are also classes for hacks and for show ponies — the latter being further divided into types and heights. In addition there are show classes for many of the different breeds of horse and pony — some to be shown in-hand (that is, without a rider) and others under saddle. Smaller shows have classes for working ponies, in which conformation plays a less important part than performance.

American shows and show classes are run along quite different lines. The classes are divided according to styles of riding as well as different breeds and types. There are also Pleasure Horse Classes, in which the horse's performance, manners, turn-out and suitability to the rider are all given greater consideration and higher marks than the

Left: *An attractively marked show pony is to be shown side-saddle by its young rider.* (Peter Roberts)

Below: *A beautiful palamino, ready for the western showing class, shows off to spectators.* (Peter Roberts)

Competitors in a Grand Prix coaching competition splash through a pond that is part of the course. This is another sport that has benefited from the patronage of the British Royal family.
(Peter Roberts)

Left: *The pony scurry driving, in which competitors race round an obstacle course, is popular with spectators and obviously fiercely competitive among these young 'coachmen'!* (Peter Roberts)

animal's conformation.

More than in any other branch of competitive equestrianism, the outcome and final placing of show horses depends on the individual preferences of the judge. Horses and ponies which find favour with one judge may be placed well down the line by another one on another day at another show.

Driving, of course, has its origins buried deep in the chariot races of the ancient world, just as harness racing does. Competition driving and harness racing, however, may be considered quite separately as they have really developed along quite different lines. Most competition driving is as close to the world of showing as to racing.

Nowadays there are several different competitive driving events ranging from light, pony pulled gigs judged on turn-out and performance, to the combined driving competitions in which pairs, four-in-hands, and sometimes even larger teams are driven in an event that involves a dressage test, a marathon cross-country drive over rough ground, up steep hills and through streams and ponds, ending with an obstacle driving test. This is popular throughout Europe and the *Fédération Equestre Internationale* officially recognizes it as a sport, and has drawn up rules for it.

All sorts of different horses are used in driving competitions, depending on the type of event. A breed of horse and pony bred specifically for driving is the showy hackney, noted for its unique high-stepping action. Hackneys, particularly ponies, always attract a large crowd when driven in the show ring. Cleveland Bays are another favourite breed with the driving fraternity. This is an ancient British breed, once much used as a packhorse, which has been considerably improved in the last couple of centuries by crossing with Thoroughbreds. German horses — Oldenburgs and Holsteins in particular — make excellent harness horses and are popular the world over.

Equestrian competition, with all the excitement and variety it offers, is perhaps the clearest example of the horse's changing role in our society.

The Sporting and Holiday Horse

100

Pages 98 & 99: *In the steer wrestling event, the cowboy slips from his galloping mount and grasps the steer by the horns, ready to wrestle it to the ground.* (US Travel Service)

Right: *An old sporting print depicts three scenes from a day's fox hunting: the meet (top), the chase (centre) and the kill (bottom).* (Mary Evans Picture Library)

Henry Alken

Henry Alken

THE MEET

FULL CRY

Finally we arrive at the Sporting and Holiday horses. There are inevitably some areas of overlap in the categories in this book as show-jumping and racing, for example, are equestrian sports as well as competitions; polo and the rodeo events are competitive as well as sporting; horses and ponies used for trekking holidays are of course 'riding' animals, and as already discussed, any horse used in the service of man, is a work animal! However, there is some validity in distinguishing between horses used in different pursuits and professions and the sporting events discussed in this chapter have a slightly different connotation to the international level competitions of the last chapter.

Perhaps the most famous or infamous sport practised by men mounted on horseback is that of hunting. Nowadays this term most generally refers to fox hunting and to a slightly lesser extent, stag and drag hunting, all effected with a pack of hounds. Drag hunting involves the laying of a line with a strong smelling substance such as aniseed over a pre-determined course, which the hounds and mounted followers then pursue.

In his time man has hunted all manner of 'wild' animals from horseback — using hounds, bows and arrows or lances and spears. Sometimes the hunting has been for necessity in order to secure food or to protect crops and livestock from predators; sometimes it has been for no other reason than for the thrill of the chase. Wild boar and oxen, hares, wolves bears, stag, bisons, tigers, lions — even elephants and giraffes — have been hunted through the ages and round the world by men mounted on horses.

Fox and stag hunting is practised in Europe, Great Britain, Canada and the United States of America, although Great Britain is undoubtedly its true home. Foxhunting is the most widely practised of all, but in fact although hunting with packs of hounds has been practised in Great Britain since the eleventh century, it was only in the

Above: *Hounds look up expectantly at their huntsman at a modern day meet.* (Peter Roberts)

Right: *Mounted followers (referred to as the 'field' in hunting parlance) splash through a pond during a hunt in Austria.* (Austrian Tourist Board)

seventeenth or eighteenth centuries that the hunting of the fox began.

Hunting was introduced into the United States of America in the late eighteenth century and was practised first in Virginia. Today, Virginia and Kentucky are the most famous hunting areas.

There is no breed of horse called a hunter, but a type of animal described as such has certainly emerged and is recognized today. In fact, there are various types of hunter suitable for differing types of terrain. In densely-ploughed country where the soil is sticky and heavy, a much stronger animal is needed than where the country consists of wide open, fast grassland. All hunters must be bold and obedient, with a willingness and ability to jump, and a temperament that is well disposed to other horses. The most famous hunter type has been bred extensively in Ireland and is known as the Irish Hunter.

Polo is one of the oldest of all equestrian sports, probably originating in the middle east in about the sixth century BC, but it did not move west to Great Britain and the United States of America until the late nineteenth century. It was army officers serving in India who were responsible for bringing the game to London.

Described as the 'fastest team game in

Right: *Polo ponies are as skilled as their riders in the tactics of the game. In this match in Dusseldorf, the ponies lean against each other in an attempt to push their opponent off course.* (ZEFA)

Below: *Polo mallets are raised high in the air in order to get as much force as possible behind the swing.* (Peter Roberts)

the world', the modern game of polo is played between two teams of four players aside. The players strike at a small ball with long wooden mallets and the aim is to score goals by hitting the ball through the goalposts of the opposing side. Most matches last about one hour and are divided into 7½-8 minute periods of play known as 'chukkas'. Because the game is conducted at a continuous gallop, most horses can only be ridden for two chukkas in each game, so a successful polo player who plays the game regularly really needs a string of polo ponies. It is this fact above all that makes it such an expensive sport in which to participate.

Polo is widely played throughout the world and because of its popularity, a type of animal, known as a polo pony, has emerged. The most successful polo ponies (which in spite of the 'pony' label usually stand about 15 hands high) are bred in Argentina. The Argentinians used to play somewhat rough and ready games of polo, using their scruffy, but remarkably agile little ranch ponies. Realizing the animal's natural aptitude for the game, they began crossing it with

Above: *A cowboy parts company from his mount during a bareback bronco riding event. The cinch strap buckled round the horse's loins makes him buck more violently.* (US Travel Service)

Right: *Although the cowboy missed the calf as he lassoed it, his horse has automatically slid to a halt in order to pit its weight against the moving calf.* (US Travel Service)

Colourful wagons hurtle round the arena in the popular chuck wagon race. (Peter Roberts)

imported Thoroughbreds, specifically to upgrade the breed and produce a better looking pony, which was then tagged a polo pony. So successful was the result, that Argentine polo ponies are widely exported round the world and have dominated the sport since the 1930s.

The rodeos first mentioned on page 17 are a sporting highlight in many parts of the United States of America, Canada and Australia. The events of most rodeos are fiercely competed and many rodeo riders are professionals who make their living by riding the 'rodeo circuit'. This is quite literally a 'make or break' existence, with huge sums of money to be made if the cowboy does not break all his bones first!

There are five traditional rodeo events. There is saddle bronc riding, in which the cowboy must remain 'in the saddle' without losing his stirrups for ten seconds and bareback bronc riding, which is similar except the horse does not wear a saddle and the rider must remain on its back for eight, doubtless interminable seconds. In calf-roping, the cowboy having lassoed the calf from the saddle, must tie it in a particular way so that it remains secure for six seconds and in bull-dogging or steer wrestling two riders participate — one riding to keep the steer in a straight line, while the other draws level with it, before leaping off his horse and wrestling the steer to the ground. Finally there is bull-riding which is the most dangerous event of all. In this a rider attempts to stay on board a twisting, bucking bull — but what makes it so dangerous is that a bull once rid of its rider will turn on him. For this reason, two mounted 'rodeo clowns' are present in the arena, their job being to distract the bull away from a fallen rider.

A famous event of some rodeos — the Calgary Stampede in Canada in particular — is the chuck wagon race. This madcap hurtle of wagons pulled by teams of four horses, swaying and lurching their way around a dusty arena to accompanying yells of encouragement from the drivers, is one of the most popular of all with spectators.

Part of the day's events at a rodeo,

too, are the gymkhana games. These more light-hearted events are also widely popular in Great Britain among members of the Pony Club. During the summer school holidays, gymkhanas are held in most rural villages and towns and the games are keenly contested by young riders astride their nippy little ponies.

There are masses of gymkhana games and different regions have their own localized variations on the well-known basic themes. One of the most traditional of all, included in the day's events at nearly all gymkhanas, is the bending race. In this, competitors race up and down a line of poles weaving their way in and out of them. This is one of the gymkhana games held at a rodeo event, too, when it is known as a barrel race — barrels replacing the poles.

Gymkhana games have become more widely popularized since the introduction of the Prince Philip Mounted Games — a team competition between Pony Clubs, the annual finals of which are held at the Horse of the Year Show in London, Each year, new and ingenious games are devised by the organizers and the event is one of the most popular of all with the crowd, all of whom are soon cheering on a particular team. Winning teams in previous years have given

Above: *A woman rider competes in the barrel race — one of the more light-hearted events at a rodeo.* (US Travel Service)

Right: *Grim determination is written on the face of this young rider as he urges his pony on in a bending race at a local gymkhana.* (Peter Roberts)

displays of their skills in various Continental cities where they were met with the same excited response.

The great advantage of gymkhana games is that almost any pony, however scruffy and suspect its breeding, can participate and be a success. It is one of the few equestrian sports where vast sums of money do not have to be spent on expensive animals and lengthy hours of specialist training.

The mounted games or skill-at-arms of the police could be described as upgraded or sophisticated gymkhana games. In fact they again spring from the training of a horse in discipline, obedience and agility for its part in battle and the training of the officer to handle a sword, lance and rifle while mounted.

Many shows have demonstrations or competitions of police skill-at-arms, but the most famous competition of all is the one held each year at the Royal Tournament in London. Here officers and horses are timed round a carefully laid-out course of small jumps, and are sometimes called on to display military skills

at the same time, shooting a balloon positioned on the top of the fence with a revolver, running through a dummy with their sword, or piercing small rings with the point of a lance. Points are given for speed, performance, style and horsemanship as well as for neatness and ability in handling the weapons. The horses used in such events are the regular mounts of the police force.

Perhaps the least attractive sport in which the horse is made to participate is that of bullfighting. It is most commonly practised in Spain, where the aim is to kill the bull, and in Portugal, where it could be said to be more a display of horsemanship than a fight to the death, for the bull is rarely killed.

The various horses used in the bullring are highly trained in obedience and usually skilled in the movements of *haute école* as well as *dressage*. Of course the dangers of an angry wild bull are always present, but few horses do sustain much injury from it. After all, the training to such an advanced level and technique is a lengthy and costly business and a bullfighter would be

Above: *Patient ponies follow their riders as they hop along frantically in another perennial favourite gymkhana game — the sack race.* (Peter Roberts)

Right: *As if being asked to pass under a striped awning is not test enough, a young volunteer clashes a pair of cymbals to upset the horse during a police skill-at-arms competition.* (Police Federation)

Left: *Andalusians are popular mounts of bull-fighters. Here they are preparing to give a display of tactics used in the bull ring.* (Peter Roberts)

Below: *The bullfighter's mount must be as brave as a lion and as agile as an athlete to allow his rider to plant the darts in the bull's neck.* (ZEFA)

reluctant to allow his mount to be put out of action if it could possibly be avoided. And it is definitely 'bad for business' if a horse gets gored, as understandably, it stirs up a quick adverse reaction from the crowd.

Horses seen in the bullring are generally of two types. Top Spanish bull-fighters, in particular, usually give a display of *haute école* before the fight, mounted on a beautiful Andalusian or Andalusian-type horse. This magnificent horse is a very old Spanish breed

whose chequered history since Roman times has resulted in a number of infusions of alien blood, so that few pure-bred Andalusians remain. The other type of horse in the ring is the one actually used in the fight and it tends to be rather finer-boned and more athletic in build than the powerfully built Andalusian. Various breeds can be used, although the horses tend to contain a fair amount of Thoroughbred blood. They, too, are very highly trained, but this time it is in the techniques of the

fight, so that they know what to do in any given situation, even before they receive an instruction from the rider.

Endurance riding is a sport that could almost be described as 'competitive' trekking or trail riding and is a comparative newcomer to the world of equestrian sports. It has become very popular, though, particularly in the United States and Australia. Endurance rides are conducted over a set course of a specified distance, usually between 80-160 kilometres (50-100 miles), which may be ridden in one day. Clearly, both horse and rider have to be extremely fit. In some places, riders wishing to participate in the longer rides have to qualify first by completing one of the shorter ones. Fairly stringent rules are laid down, at least for the long rides, mostly aimed at making sure a horse is not over-taxed, and regular veterinary checks are undertaken during the ride. If a horse does not pass one of these, the rider must drop out of the ride. Awards are given according to the average speed of horse and rider over the ride (but the average speed under British Horse Society rules is not expected to exceed 14 kilometres: 9 miles per hour) and according to the marks given at the veterinary checks.

The most famous endurance ride in the United States is the Tevis Cup, in which riders cover 160 kilometres (100 miles) through the Sierra Nevada; in Britain it is the 120-kilometre (75-mile) Golden Horseshoe Ride held at a variety of venues, and in Australia it is the Quilty Ride which traverses 160 kilometres (100 miles) of the beautiful Blue Mountains in New South Wales.

Again, any type of horse can participate, but it must exceed 14 hands high and be at least five years old. Successful horses are those endowed with excessive stamina and endurance as well as sure-footedness and soundness. Arabians and Anglo-Arabs are consistently successful in all three countries.

The use of the horse as a holiday animal is undoubtedly a phenomenon of the twentieth century and more particularly the post-war years. Since then, all manner of equestrian holidays have been devised and many people quite literally

Left: *Pony trekkers in Austria ride the country's native Haflinger ponies. These ponies are almost always chestnut-coloured with a flaxen mane and tail.* (Peter Roberts)

Above: *Riders prepare for a ride through the fells from a trekking centre in Cumbria.* (C. A Visual)

Previous page: *Trail riders pass through sun-baked country in Arizona. Spiky cacti tower above them, pointing towards an azure blue sky.* (US Travel Service)

spend their vacations in the saddle. All horse-orientated countries of the world offer riding holidays of some sort and for many of them, there is no need even to be a proficient rider to enjoy one's holiday in this way.

Pony-trekking is probably the pastime most commonly associated with a riding holiday, but the term covers a multitude of meanings. Some hotel or holiday centres offering trekking as part of their activities refer to no more than an hour or two's ride a day around the surrounding district. Other trekking holidays fall into two main groups — those where day-long rides go out from the centre, covering new ground each day but returning to the same spot to sleep each night, and those where the whole

holiday is 'one long ride' in that riders go from one place to the next, riding all day and stopping overnight in different venues along the route. These stops are all fixed well in advance by the riding establishment or trekking centre.

Horses and ponies used for trekking are usually 'patent-safe' mounts, well used to having virtual novice riders on their backs. Most countries, and regional districts therein, will use the ponies of the area, hence trekking centres in Exmoor and Dartmoor use the moorland ponies, as those in Wales use Welsh Mountain ponies and those in Scotland use Highland ponies. In Iceland where trekking holidays are extremely popular, the comfortable little Icelandic ponies are the obvious

Left: *A splash in the cool, shallow waters of a lake makes a welcome respite for ponies on a long, hot day's trek.* (ZEFA)

Below: *Non-skiers may prefer to enjoy their winter holiday relaxing in a horse-drawn sleigh.* (Peter Roberts)

choice, while in Austria and Bavaria it is often the hard-working little native Haflinger ponies that get the job. In Norway, it is the ancient breed of Fjord pony, which picks its way along the rugged mountain paths with the agility of a mountain goat, that is most frequently used.

In the United States, trail riding is similar to trekking and varies in practice in much the same way. Some rides may be no more than a few people enjoying a quiet hack for a couple of hours or they may be huge organized affairs in which a hundred or more riders take part over a period of perhaps two weeks. In such instances, riders usually camp out at night, so besides being good horsemen, used to spending hours and days in the saddle, they also have to be well versed in what equipment to take for themselves and their mount for this length of time. Most such rides come under the auspices of some organization, such as the American Forest Association, which has a division called Trail Riders of the Wilderness. They usually limit their number of riders to about thirty, assuming that most will take two horses (riding one and leading one to carry the equipment). The rides go across such places as the Saw Tooth Wilderness in Idaho and the Pecos Wilderness of New Mexico.

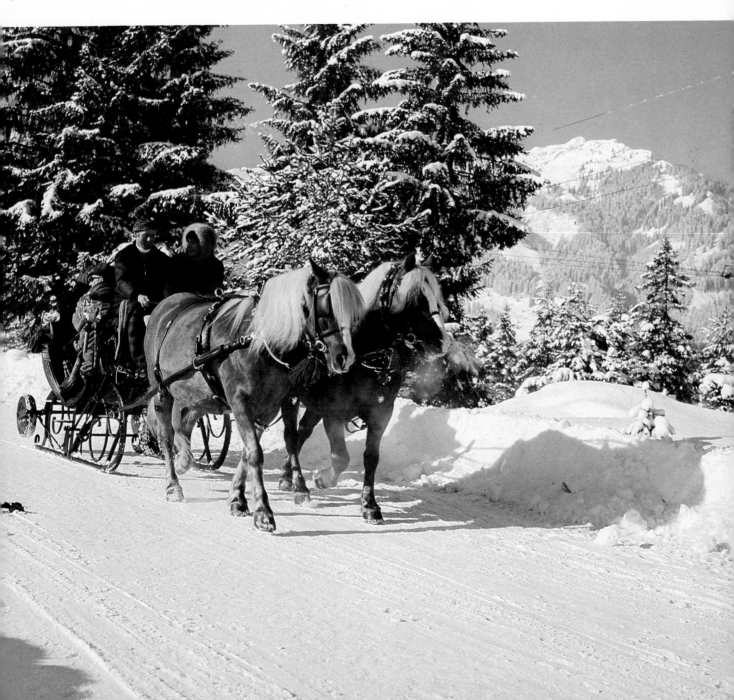

Left: *A welcome drink from a leaf-strewn water trough for this horse, pulling a family of holiday-makers through the Jura region of Switzerland.* (Peter Roberts)

Under the bright lights at the finale of the Horse of the Year Show in London, these magnificent horses give meaning to Ronald Duncan's moving tribute. (Peter Roberts)

Modern trail riding, purely recreational as it is, originated from the famous Western Cattle Drives and the pre-mechanized era before proper roads were built, when to ride along the 'trails' was the only way to get from one place to another. Some trail rides still involve cattle drives as part of the attraction.

Not all equestrian holidays involve riding, however. In Switzerland, as in other countries, those who enjoy caravanning can take a step backwards in time, but still indulge this hobby, by hiring a horse-drawn covered wagon for the duration of their holiday. (Tuition in driving is given at the start!) Denmark has come up with a clever idea for families including both riders and non-riders who want to spend their holidays together. The riders join a trekking group, while the non-riders accompany them in a horse-drawn vehicle, driven in this instance by one of the holiday organizers.

In many holiday fêtes and carnivals the horse contributes to the pomp and pageantry of the occasion by being dressed up in some traditional gear.

All in all, when one considers how much of man's life the horse has shared over the centuries — his mundane daily toil, his travels and migrations, his joys and sorrows, his victories and defeats — it is no wonder that he is now also becoming an integral part of so many people's annual holiday. And it adds yet another dimension to Ronald Duncan's moving tribute spoken each year on the final night of the Horse of the Year Show in London:

> Where in this wide world can a man find nobility without pride, friendship without envy or beauty without vanity? Here: where grace is laced with muscle and strength by gentleness confined.
> He serves without servility; he has fought without enmity. There is nothing so powerful, nothing less violent; there is nothing so quick, nothing more patient. England's past has been borne on his back. All our history is his industry. We are his heirs; he our inheritance.
>
> The Horse.